HUMAN BODY BOOK

INTRODUCTION TO THE VASCULAR SYSTEM

Children's Anatomy & Physiology Edition

Speedy Publishing LLC
40 E. Main St. #1156
Newark, DE 19711
www.speedypublishing.com

The vascular system is centered on the heart.

The vascular system, also called the circulatory system, is made up of the vessels that carry blood and lymph through the body.

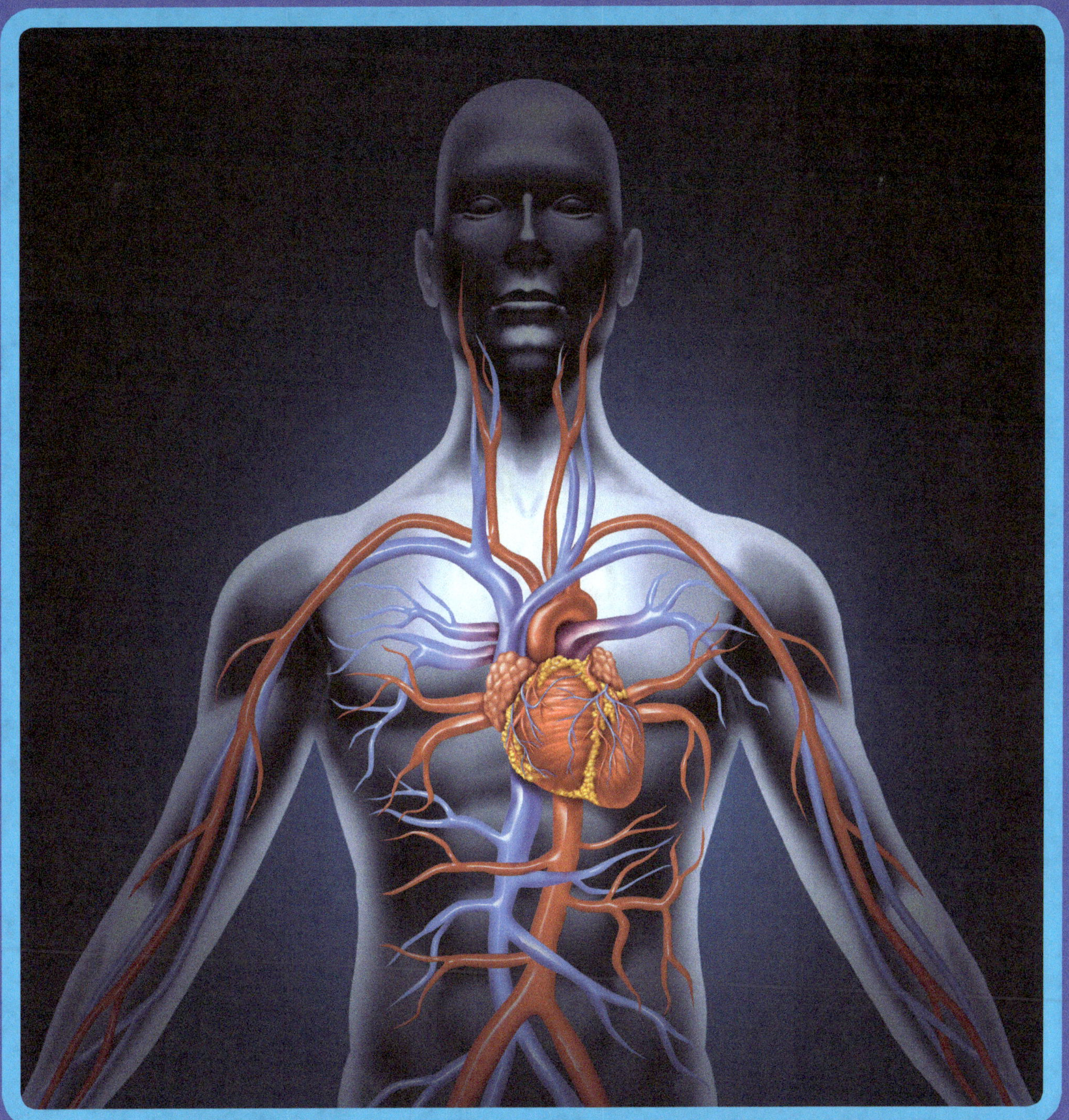

The arteries and veins carry blood throughout the body, delivering oxygen and nutrients to the body tissues and taking away tissue waste matter.

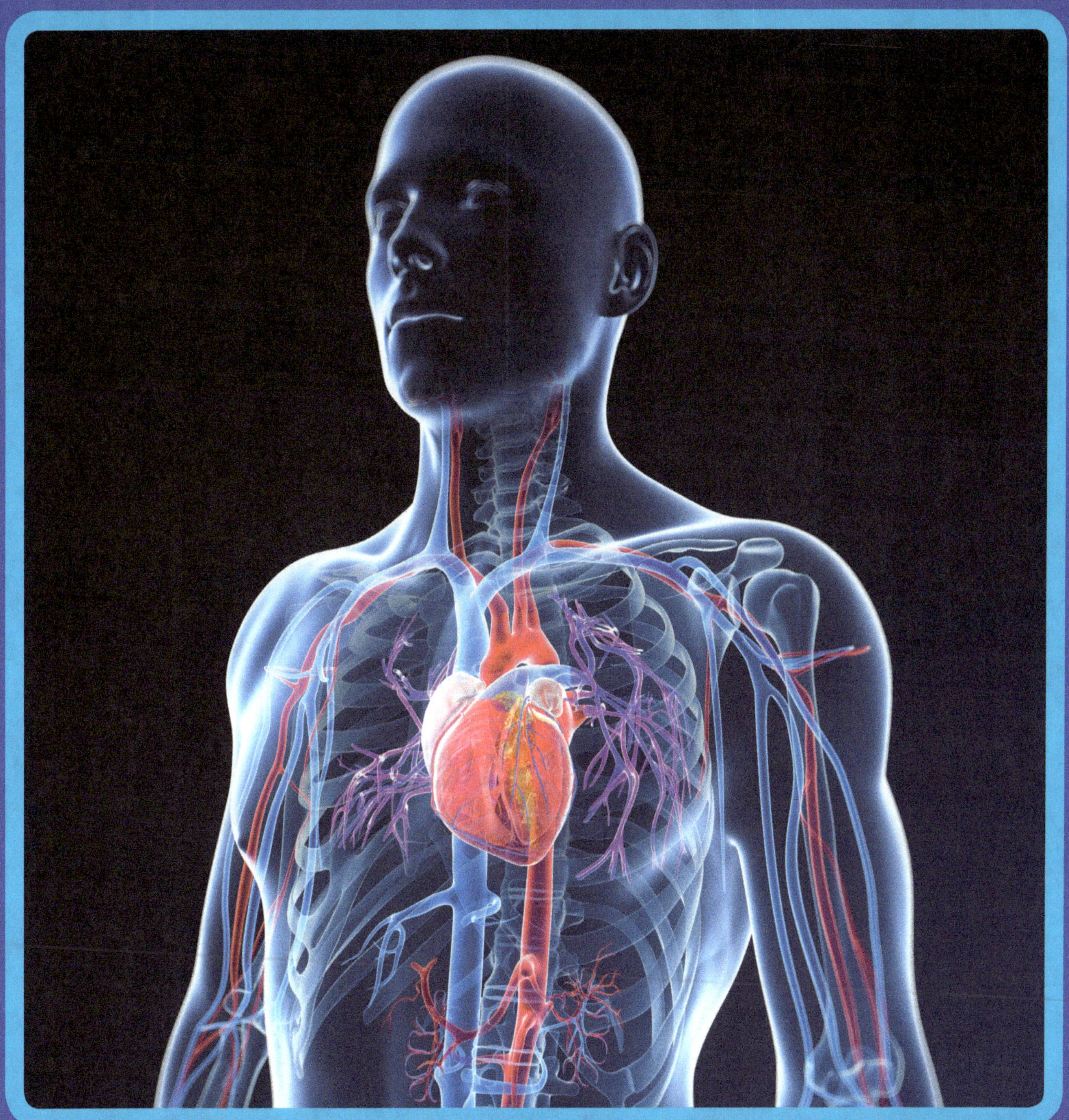

The essential components of the human vascular system are the heart, blood and blood vessels.

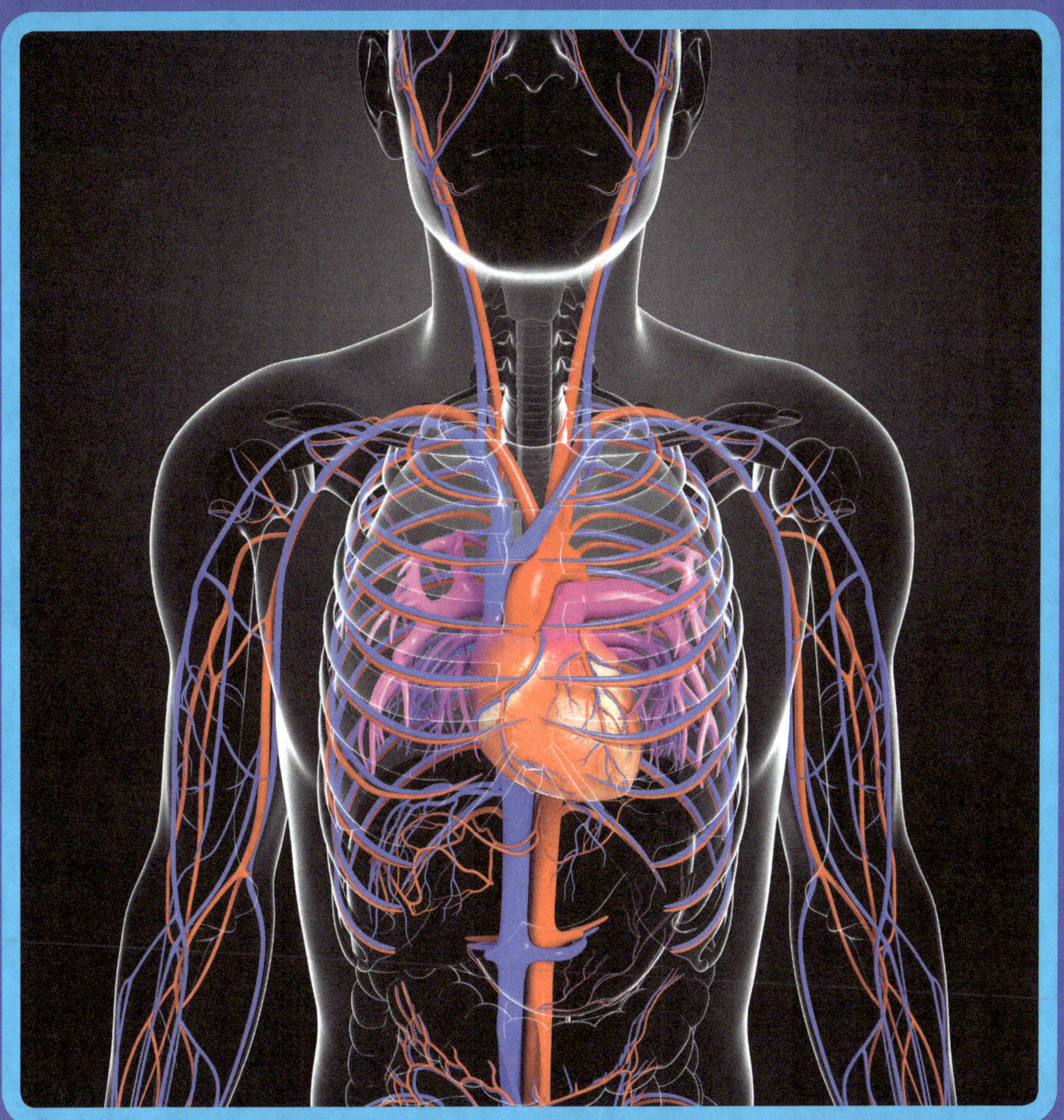

Without the circulatory system, the body would not be able to fight disease or maintain a stable internal environment.

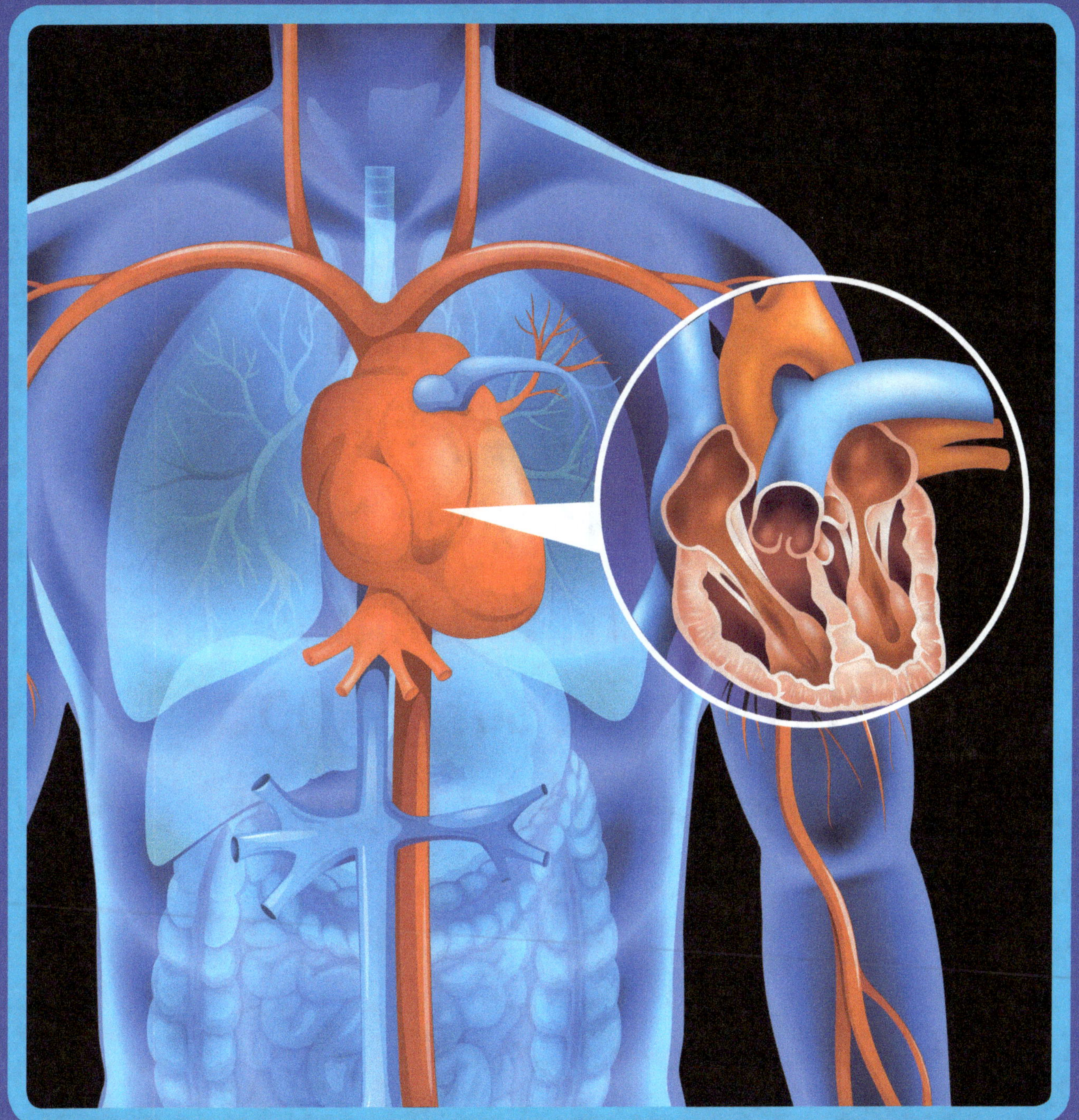

Every day, the approximately 5 liters of blood in your body travel many times through about 60,000 miles of blood vessels.

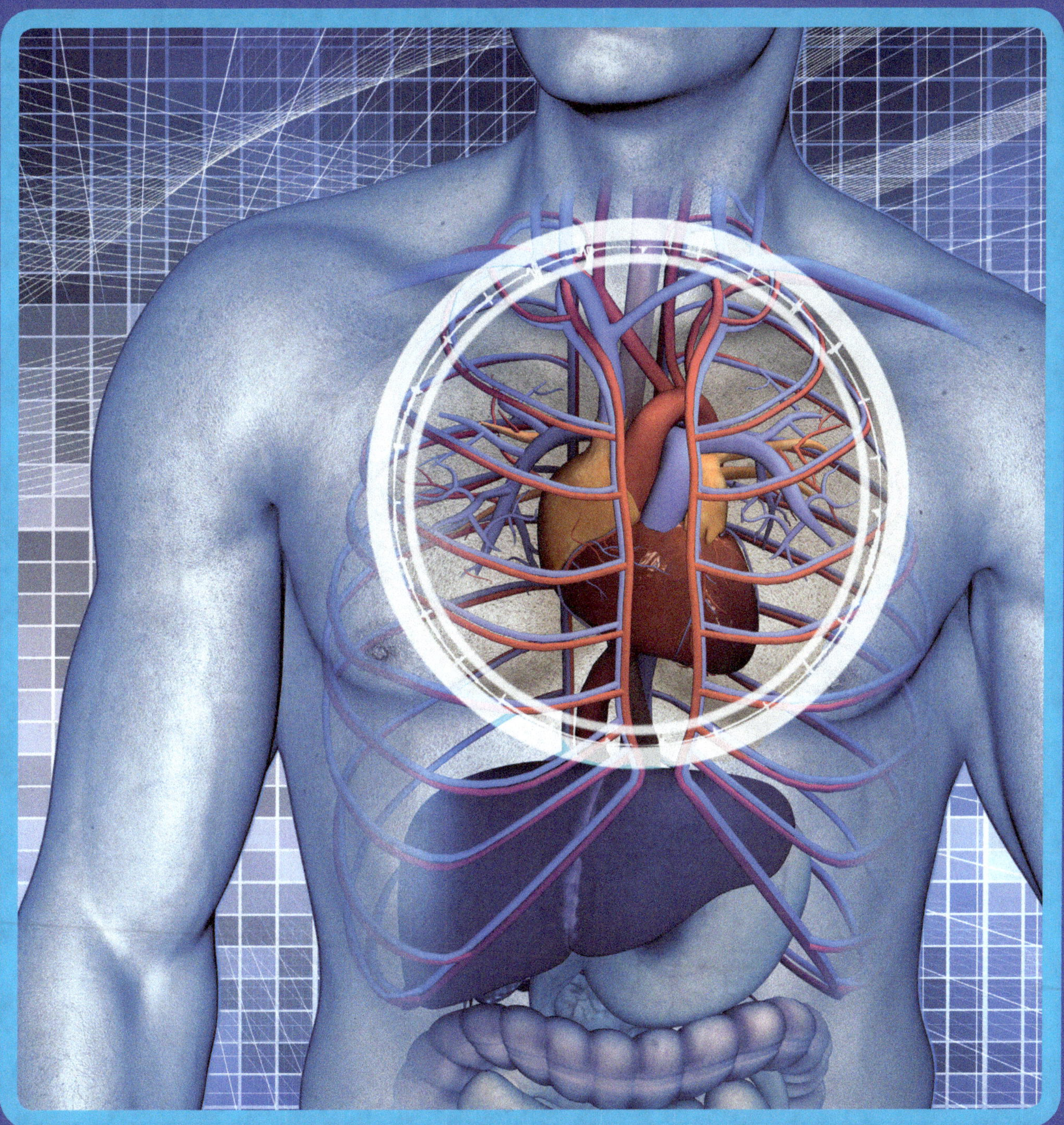

The heart is the key organ in the circulatory system.

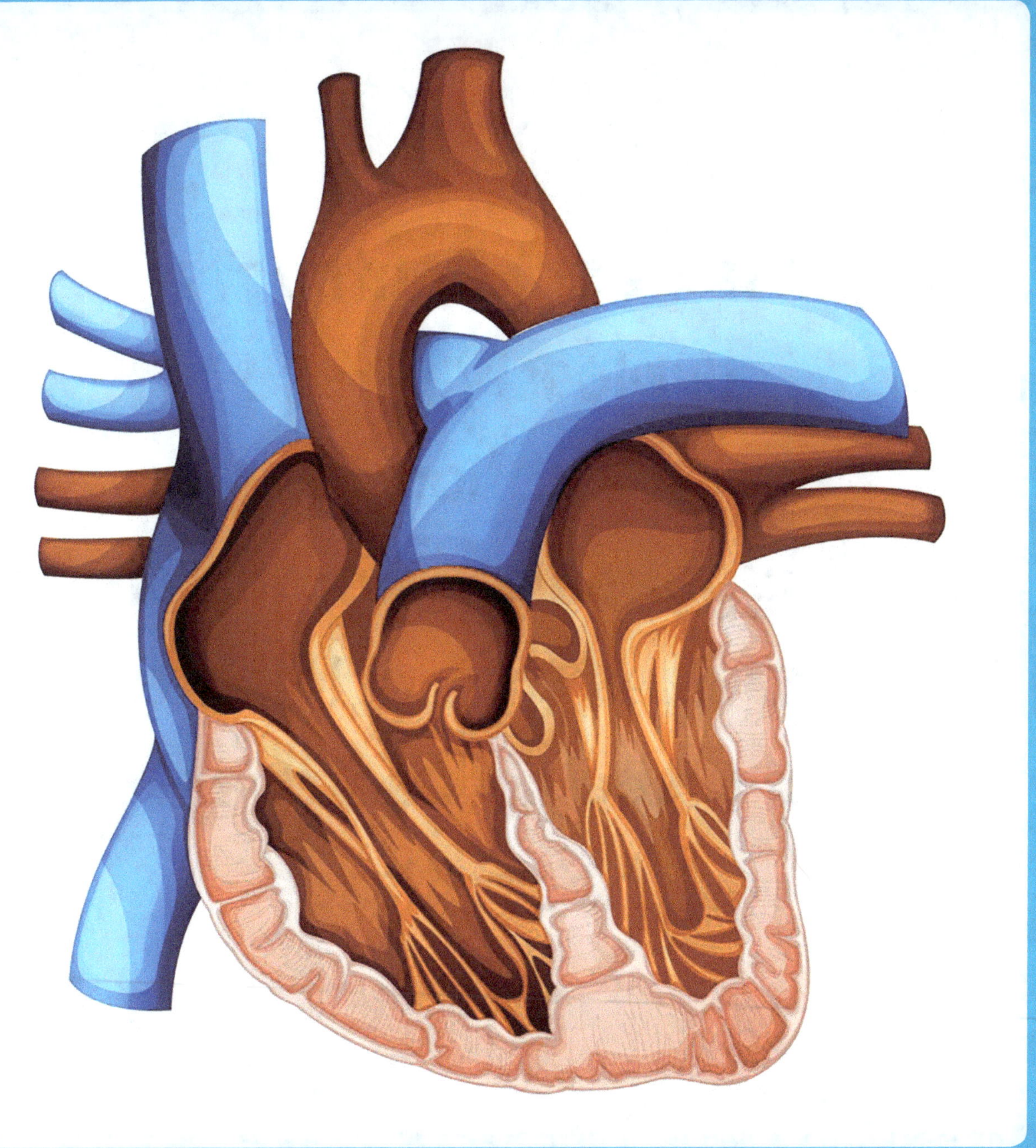

The heart contracts tirelessly, these contractions are triggered by electrical impulses that originate in a specialized area of heart tissue.

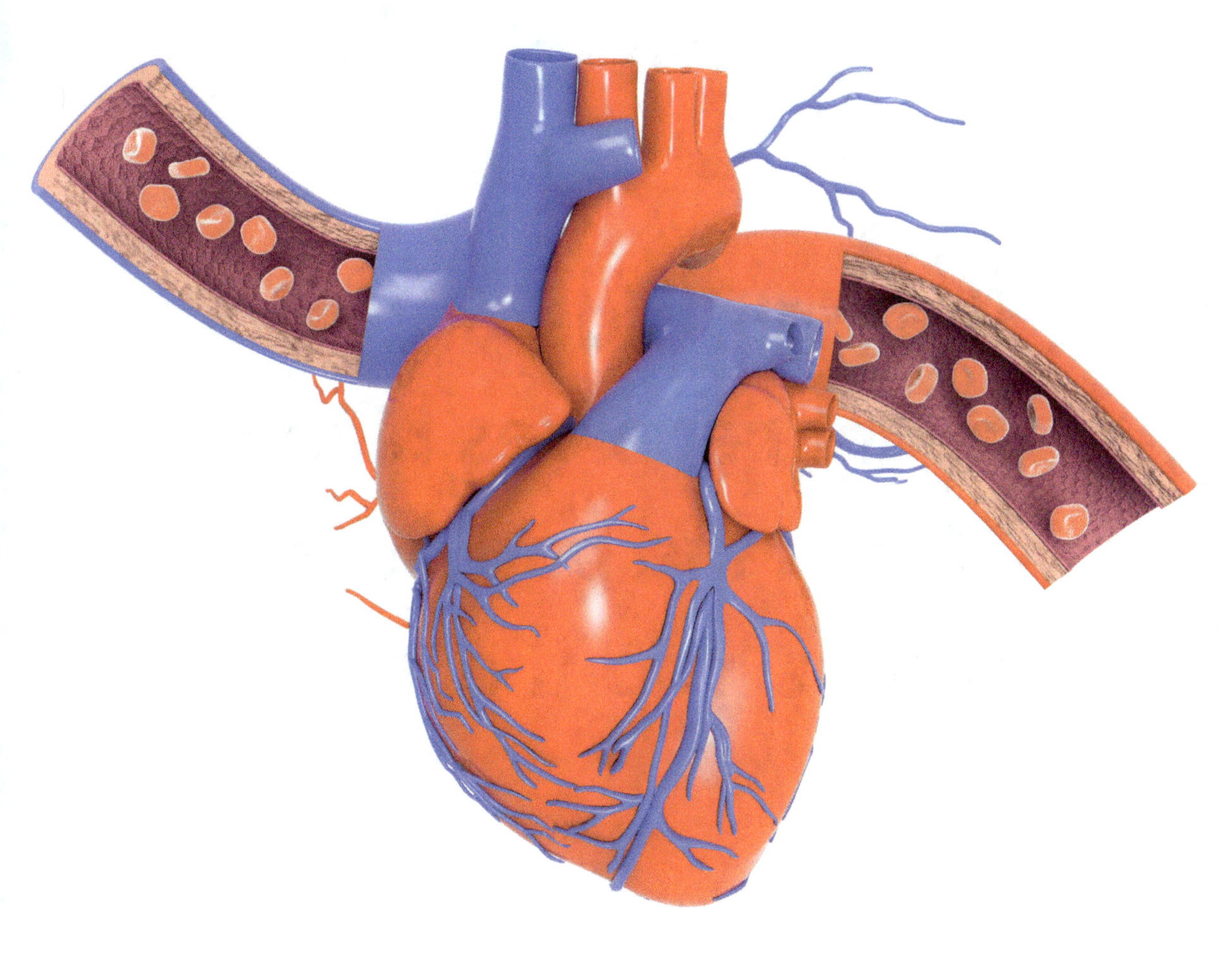

The right side of your heart receives blood from the body and pumps it to the lungs.

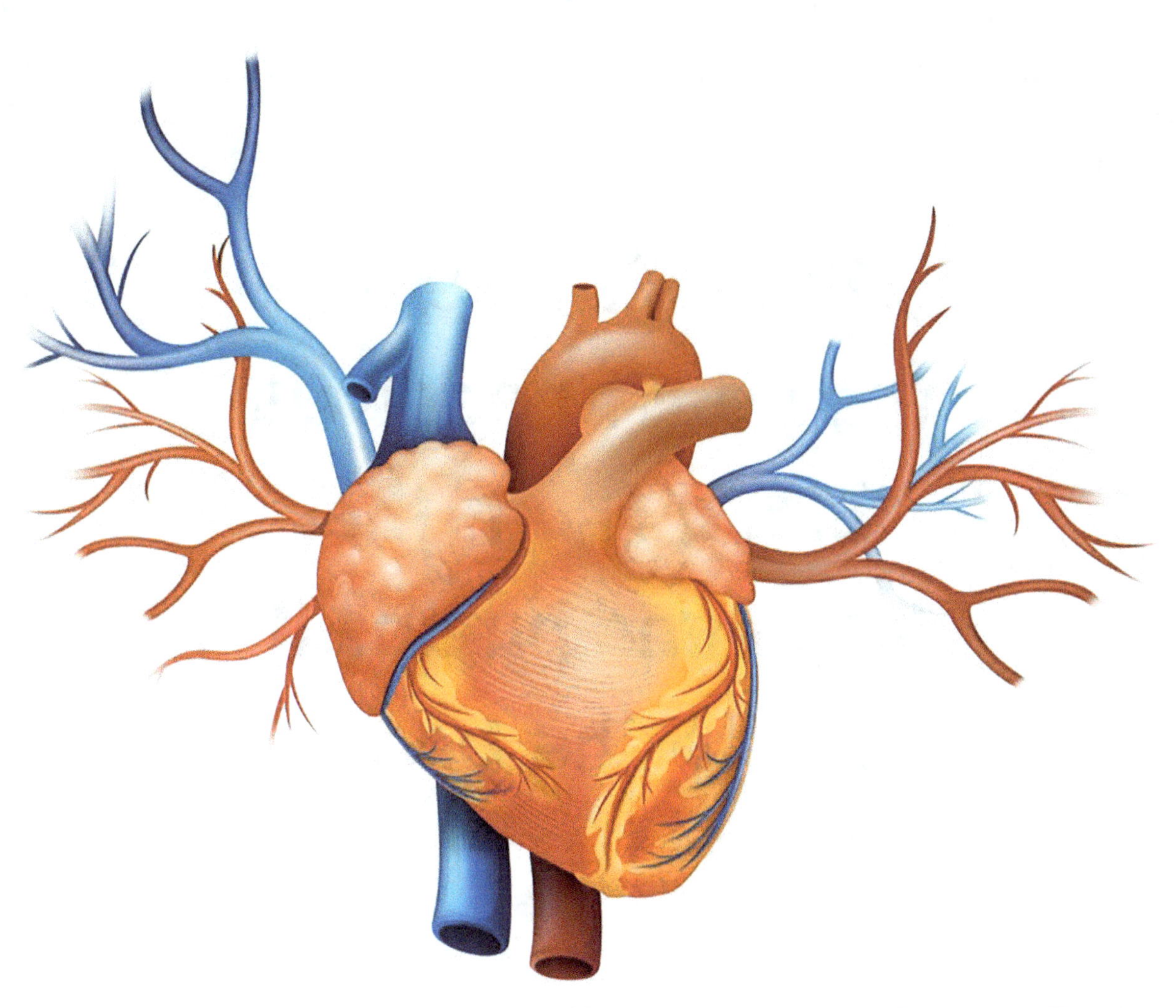

The left side of the heart receives blood from the lungs and pumps it out to the body.

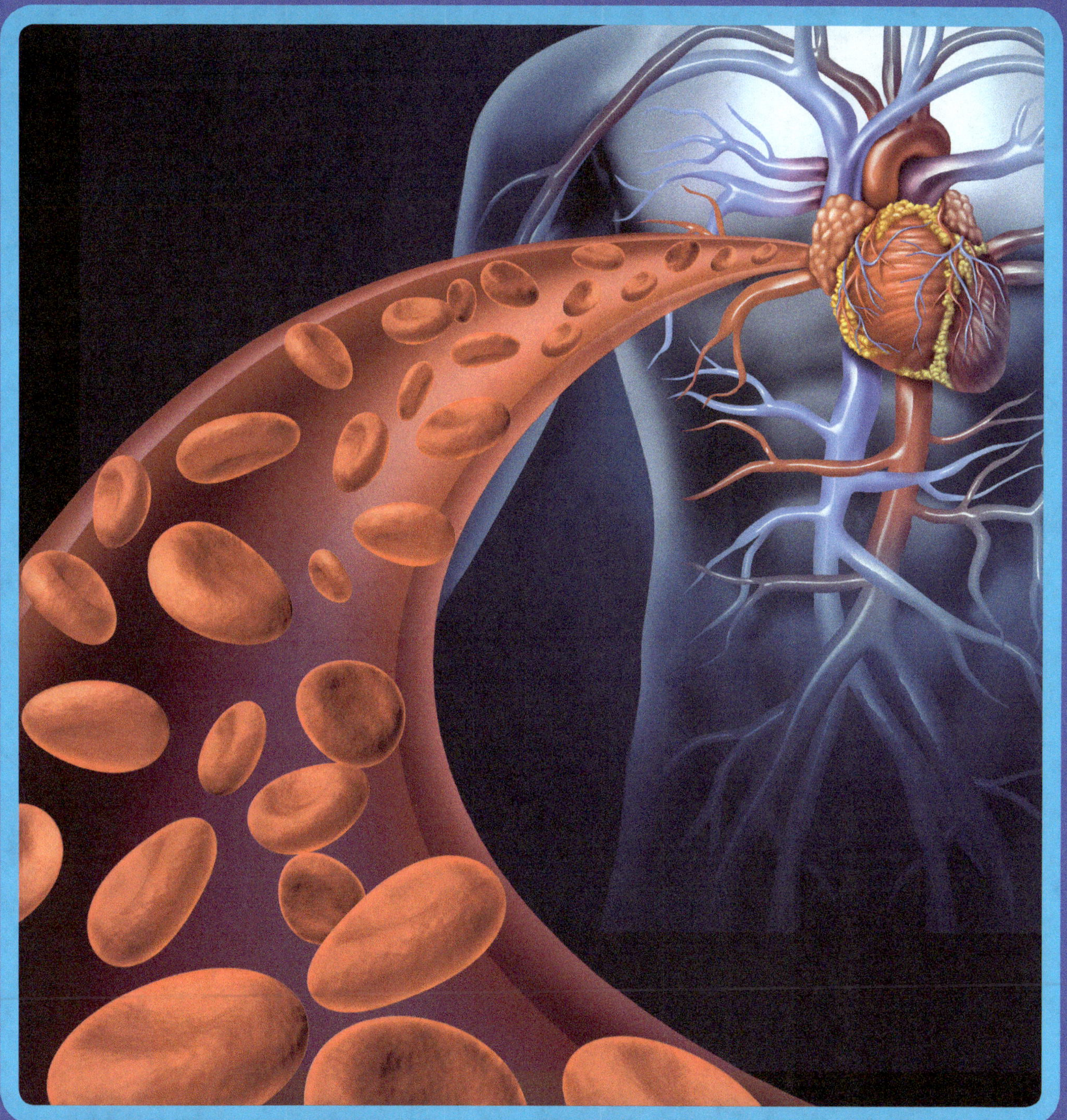

Veins and arteries are known as blood vessels.

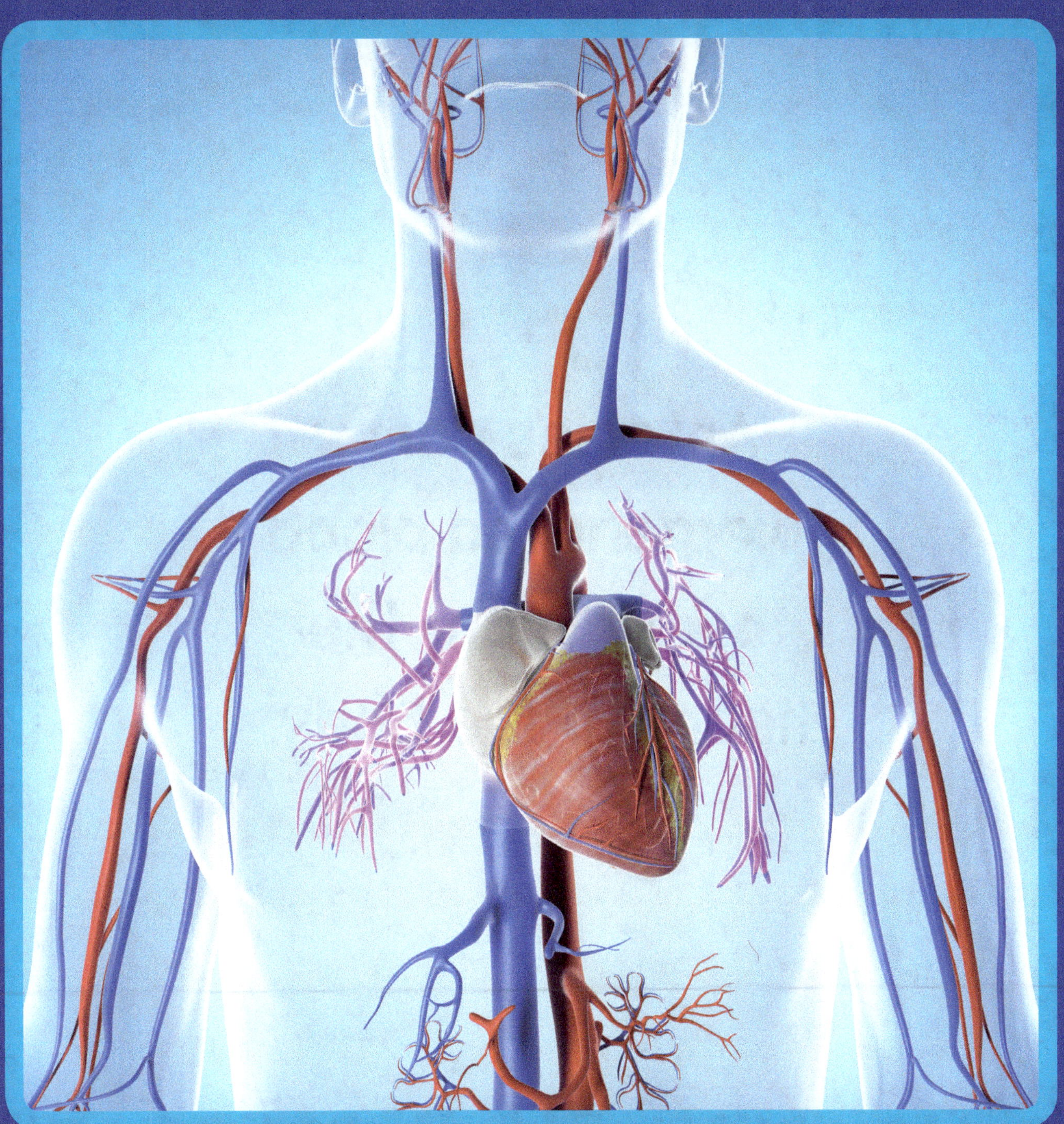

Arteries carry oxygenated blood away from the heart to the body.

Arteries have a higher blood pressure than other parts of the circulatory system.

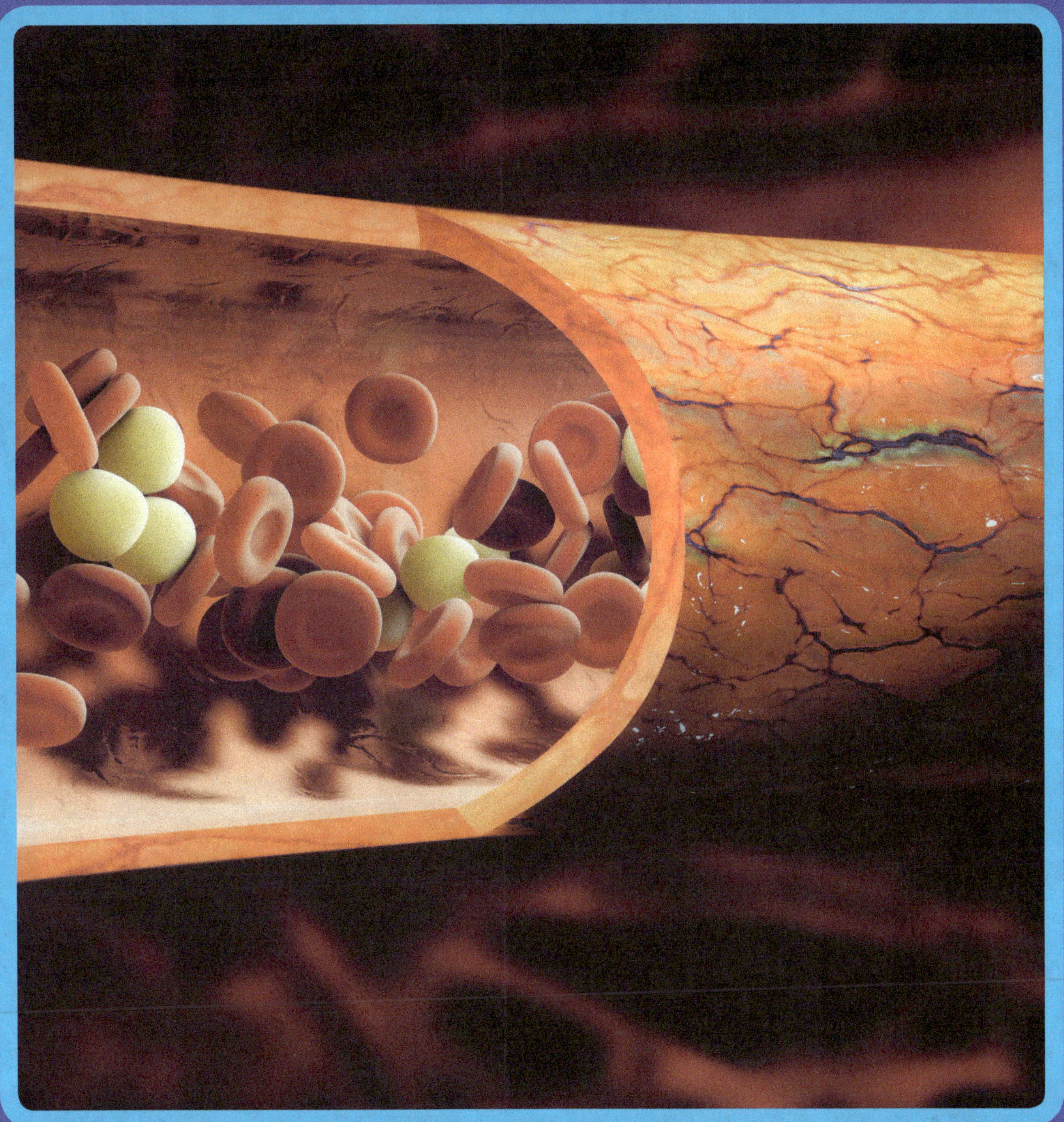

Veins carry blood from the body back into the heart.

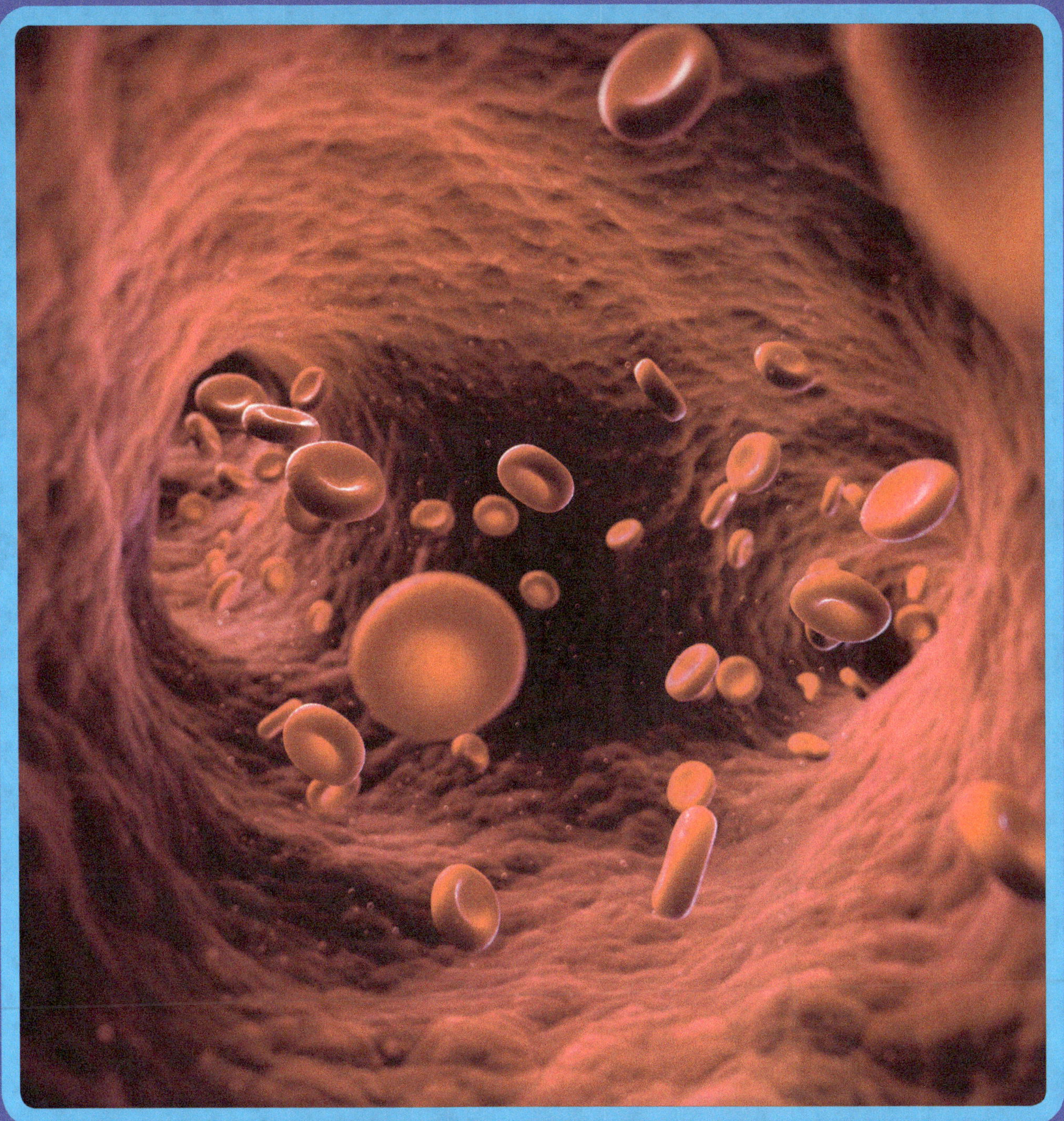

Most veins carry deoxygenated blood from the tissues.

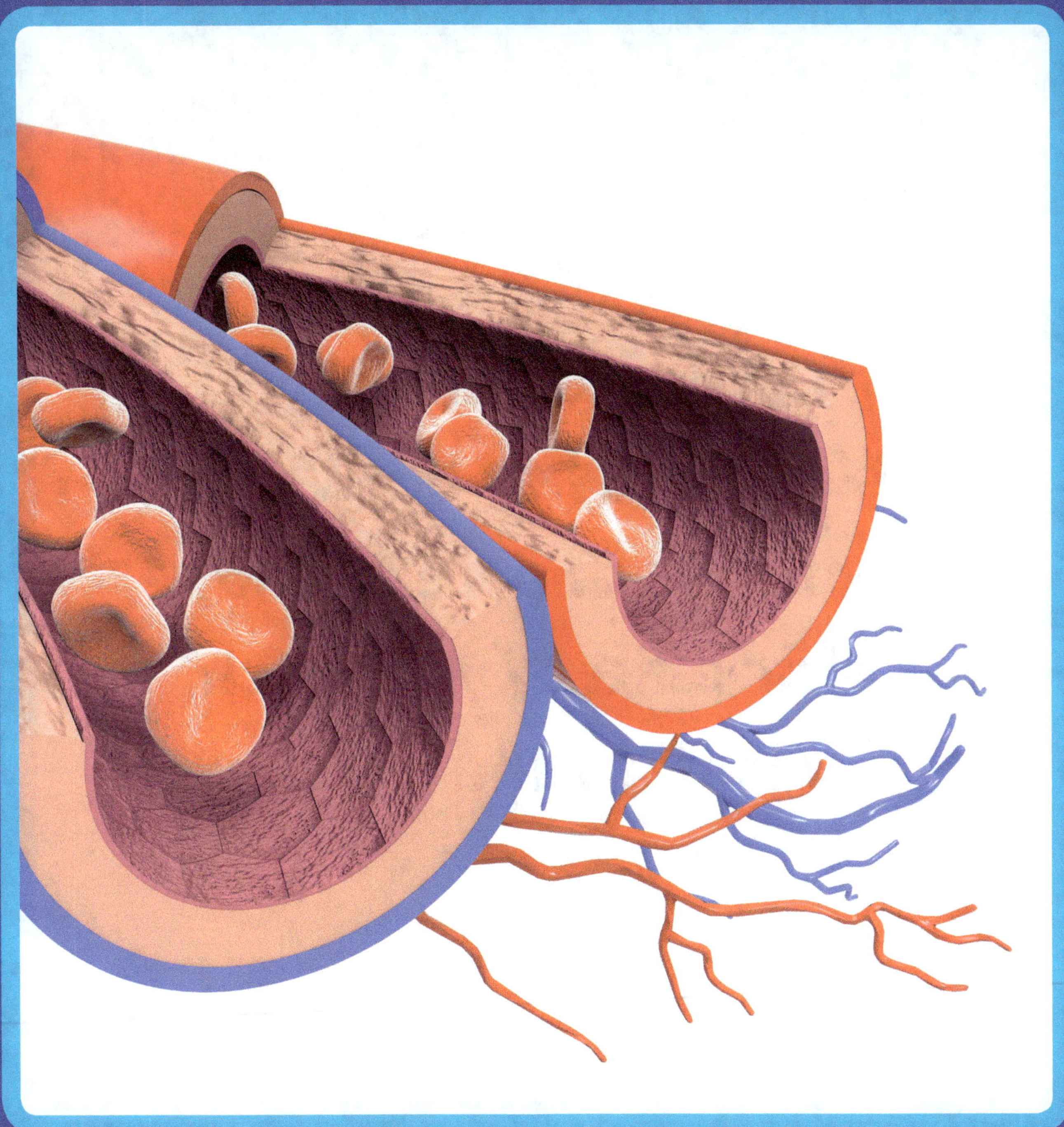

Capillaries are tiny blood vessels between arteries and veins that distribute oxygen-rich blood to the body.

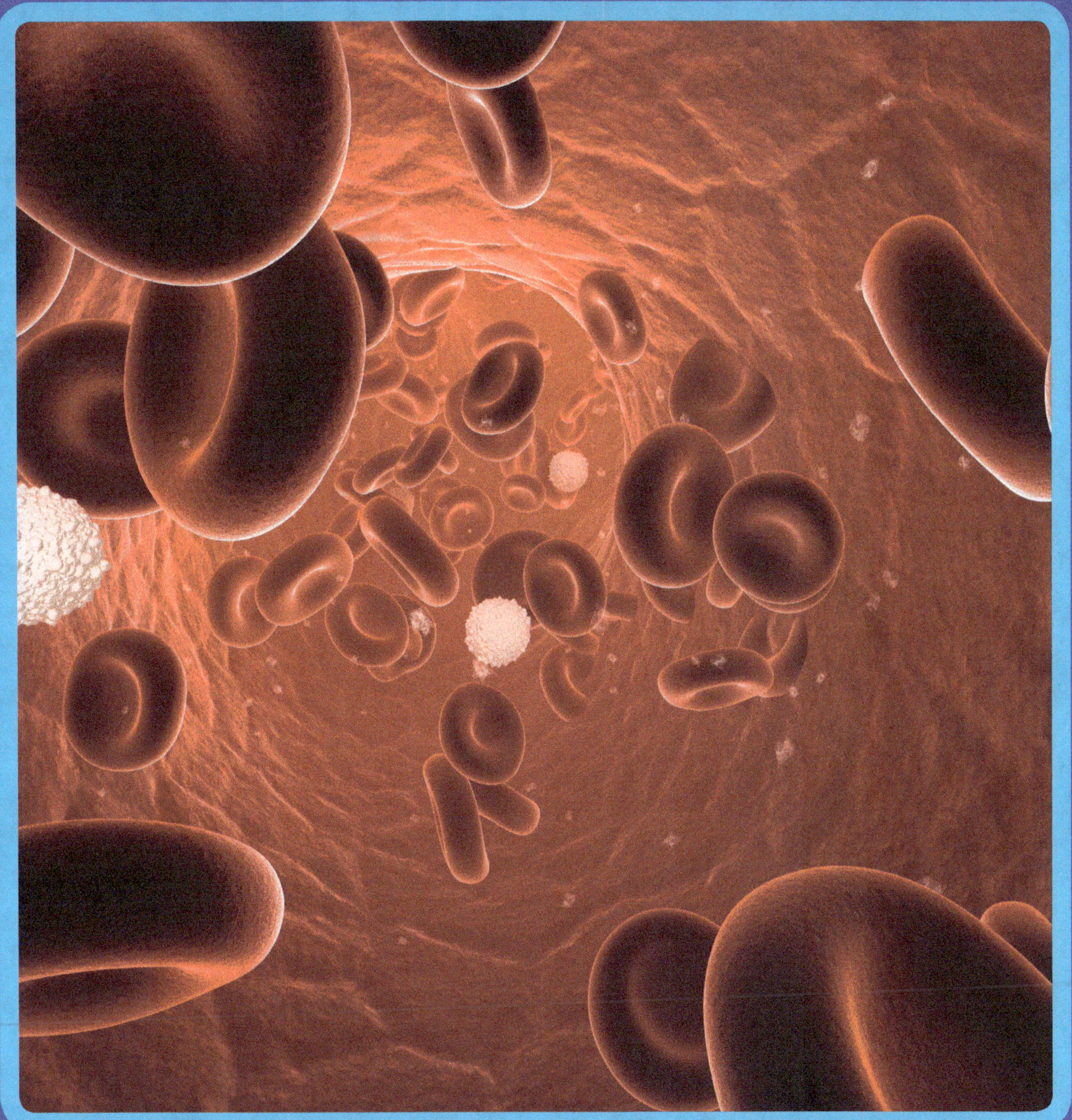

Blood is composed of a straw-coloured fluid, plasma, and huge numbers of blood cells that float in the plasma.

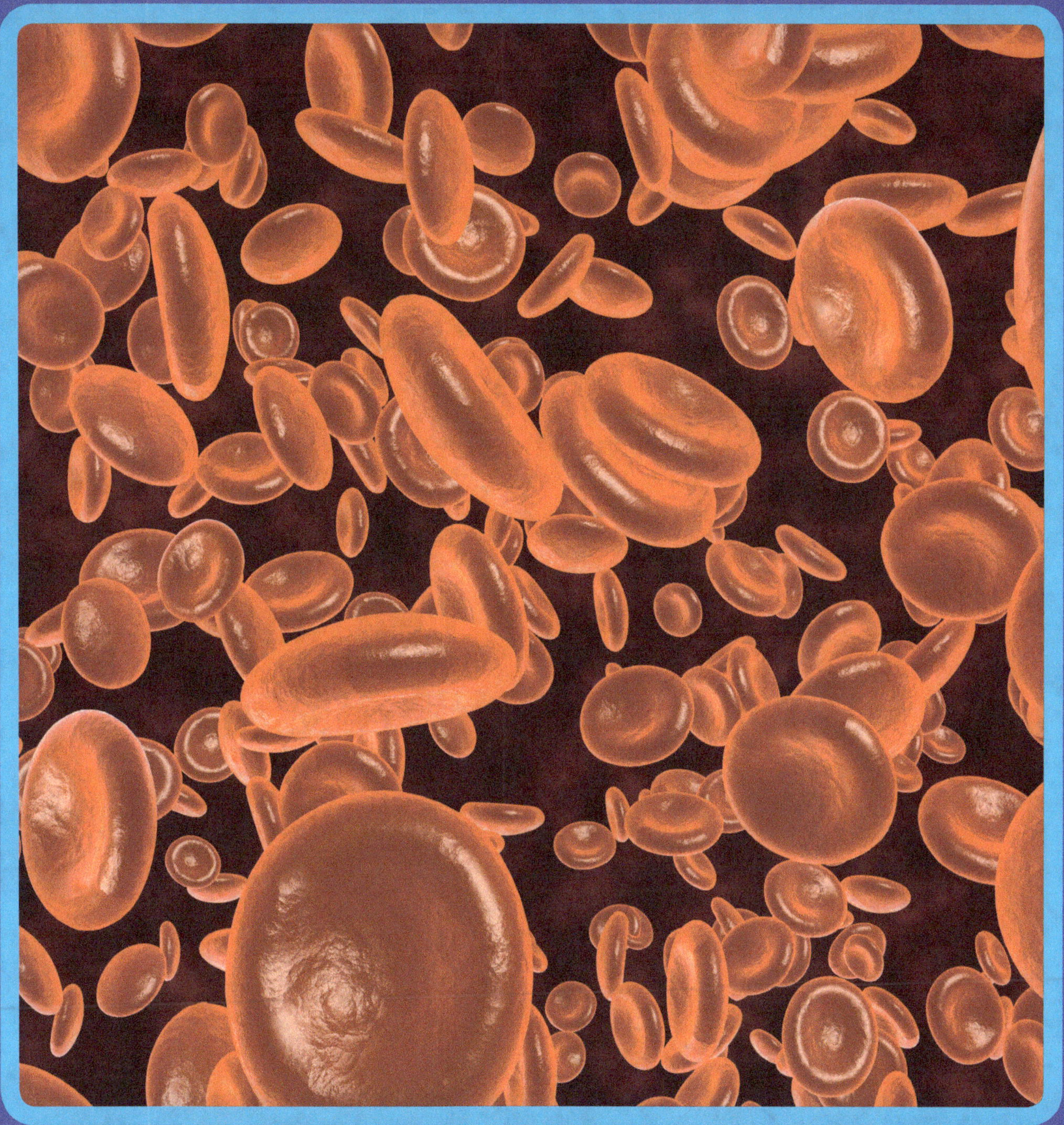

If a blood vessel is damaged, a clot forms to stop blood leaking. The solid clot remains until the blood vessel has been repaired.

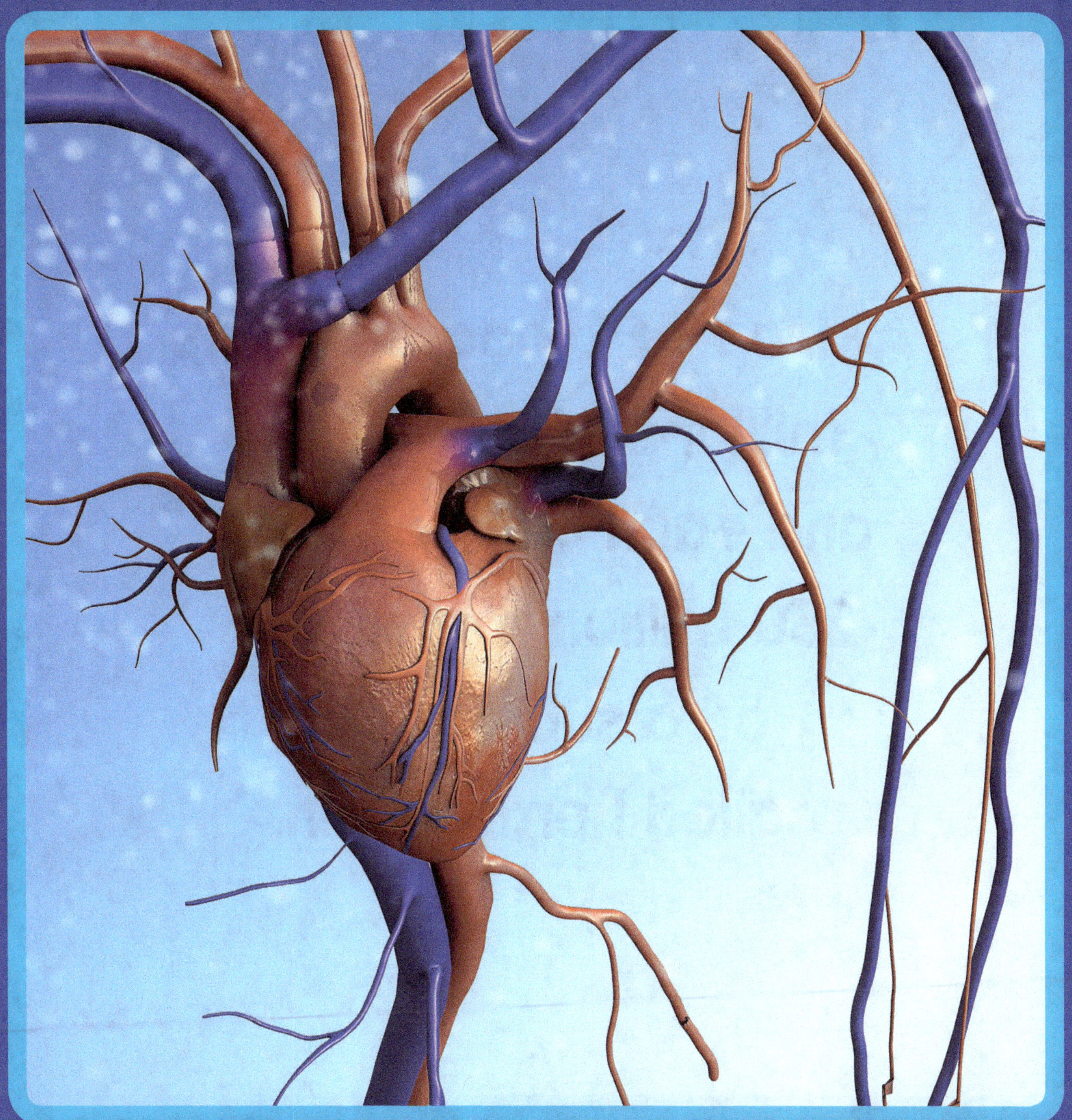

A drop of blood contains millions of red cells, and each cell contains 250 million molecules of a substance called hemoglobin.

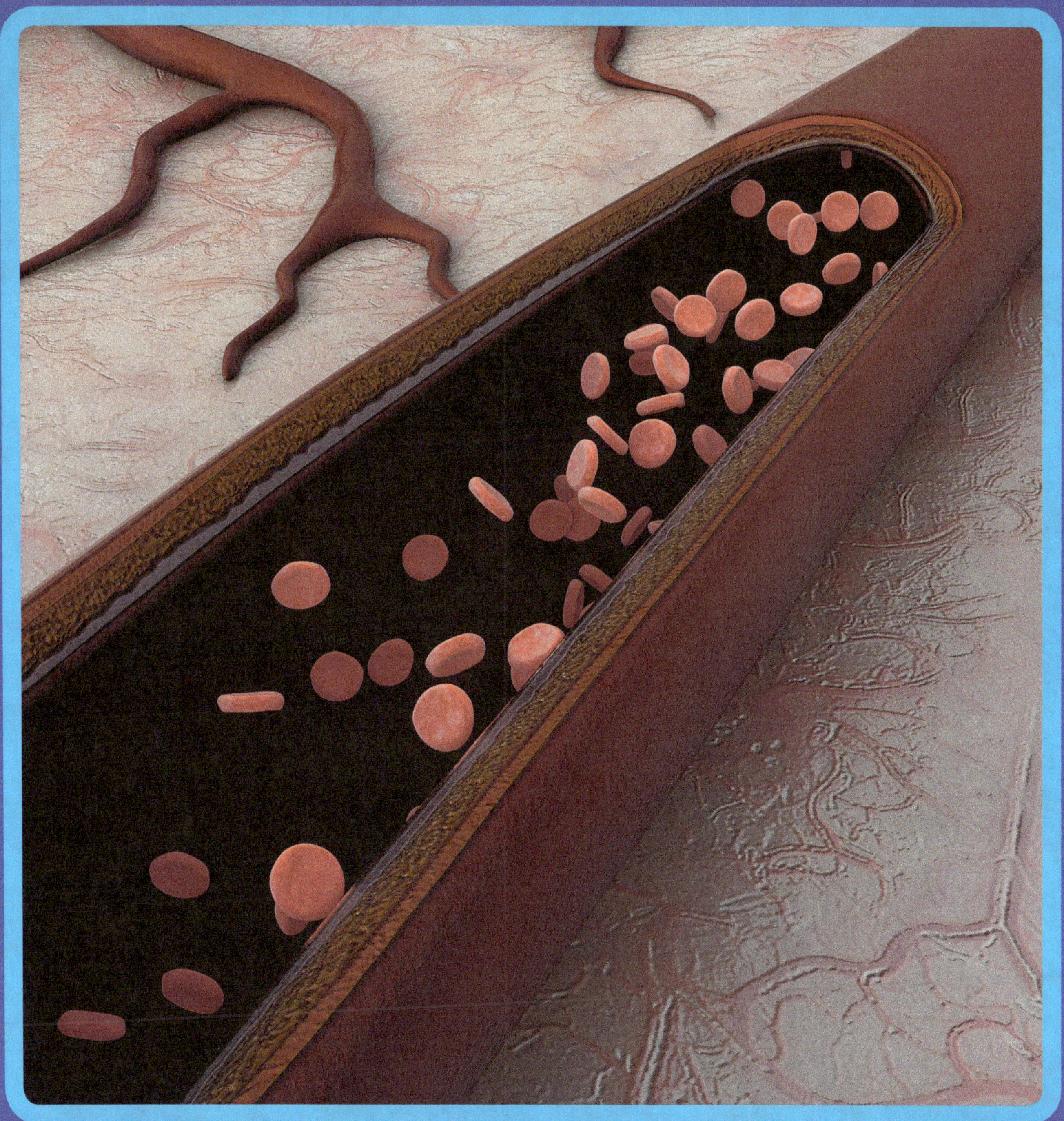

Visit
BABY PROFESSOR
EDUCATION KIDS
www.BabyProfessorBooks.com
to download Free Baby Professor eBooks
and view our catalog of new and exciting
Children's Books

www.ingramcontent.com/pod-product-compliance
Lightning Source LLC
LaVergne TN
LVHW060511170826
845677LV00026B/1718